The Gospel of Judas

*The Lost Teachings of Divine Mystery
and Enlightenment*

A Modern Translation

Adapted for the Contemporary Reader

Judas Iscariot
(Gnostic Tradition)

Translated by Tim Zengerink

© **Copyright 2025**
All rights reserved.

It is not legal to reproduce, duplicate, or transmit any part of this document in either electronic means or in printed format. Recording of this publication is strictly prohibited and any storage of this document is not allowed unless with written permission from the publisher except for the use of brief quotations in a book review.

This book contains works of fiction. Any resemblance to persons living or dead, or places, events, or locations is purely coincidental.

Table Of Contents

Preface - Message to the Reader 1

Introduction 5

    The Lost Teachings of Divine Mystery and
        Enlightenment 5

    Rediscovery and Historical Context 6

    Judas Iscariot Reimagined 6

    Exploring Gnostic Mysticism 7

    Themes and Teachings 8

    Modern Relevance and Translation 9

    Embarking on Your Journey 10

    A Call to Enlightenment 11

Jesus Criticizes the Disciples 12

    Another Generation 14

    The Disciples' Vision 15

    Jesus and Judas 18

    Jesus Reveals Everything to Judas 21

    The Betrayal 25

Thank You for Reading 28

Preface - Message to the Reader

What If You Could Help Rebuild the Greatest Library in Human History?

Thousands of years ago, the Library of Alexandria stood as the crown jewel of human achievement — a sanctuary where the collected wisdom of every known civilization was gathered, preserved, and shared freely.

And then, it was lost.

Through fire, conquest, and the slow erosion of time, humanity lost not just books — but ideas, dreams, discoveries, and stories that could have changed the world forever.

Today, the Library of Alexandria lives again — and you are invited to be a part of its restoration.

Our mission is simple yet profound:

To rebuild the greatest library the world has ever known, and to translate all timeless works into every language and dialect, so that no seeker of knowledge is ever left behind again.

Translated by Tim Zengerink

By joining our movement to rebuild the modern Library of Alexandria, you become part of an unprecedented mission:

- **Unlimited Access to the Greatest Audiobooks & eBooks Ever Written**

    Instantly explore thousands of legendary works—Plato, Shakespeare, Jane Austen, Leo Tolstoy, and countless more. All instantly available to read or listen, placing a complete literary universe at your fingertips.

- **Beautiful Paperback & Deluxe Editions at Printing Cost**

    Own any title as an elegant paperback, deluxe hardcover, or stunning collectible boxset—offered to you at true printing cost, delivered straight to your door. Build your personal Library of Alexandria, crafted for beauty, built for durability, and worthy of proud display.

- **Fresh Translations for Modern Readers—in Every Language & Dialect**

    Enjoy timeless masterpieces reimagined in clear, contemporary language—no more outdated phrases or obscure references. Alongside the original versions, we're tirelessly translating these classics into every language and dialect imaginable, ensuring accessibility and understanding across cultures and generations.

- **Join a Global Renaissance of Literature & Knowledge**

  You directly support expanding our library, publishing deluxe editions at true cost, translating works into all global languages, and bringing humanity's greatest stories to people everywhere. By joining today, you're not just preserving a legacy of masterpieces; you set in motion a powerful wave of literary accessibility.

Become a Torchbearer of Knowledge.

Join us for free now at **LibraryofAlexandria.com**

Together, we will ensure that the light of human wisdom never fades again.

With gratitude and a shared love of knowledge,

The Modern Library of Alexandria Team

Visit:

www.libraryofalexandria.com

Or scan the code below:

Introduction

The Lost Teachings of Divine Mystery and Enlightenment

Throughout Christian history, few figures have been as enigmatic, controversial, and misunderstood as Judas Iscariot. Traditionally cast as the archetype of betrayal, Judas has long embodied treachery and disloyalty in religious narratives, literature, and art. Yet, in the rediscovery of The Gospel of Judas, found in a 20th-century Coptic manuscript, we encounter an entirely different portrayal—one that radically challenges traditional beliefs and invites profound reflection on the nature of faith, divine purpose, and the spiritual mysteries of early Christianity.

The Gospel of Judas is not merely an alternative account; it is a transformative text, presenting Judas Iscariot not as a betrayer, but as a chosen disciple entrusted by Jesus himself with a sacred and essential mission. Through its bold reinterpretation, this ancient manuscript beckons readers toward a deeper exploration of early Christian mysticism, Gnostic teachings, and profound spiritual wisdom often hidden beneath surface narratives.

Translated by Tim Zengerink

Rediscovery and Historical Context

The Gospel of Judas resurfaced dramatically in the late 20th century, found within a papyrus codex discovered near El Minya in Egypt during the 1970s. After decades of clandestine dealings and scholarly restoration, the manuscript was finally authenticated and made public in 2006, reshaping our understanding of the diversity and complexity of early Christianity. Its revelation stunned the scholarly world, igniting vigorous debate and opening new avenues for theological inquiry and spiritual reflection.

This gospel belongs to the rich tapestry of Gnostic literature—texts characterized by their emphasis on hidden knowledge, spiritual awakening, and mystical insights. Originating around the second century CE, the text was likely written by members of a Gnostic community, deeply committed to uncovering and transmitting esoteric wisdom about the nature of reality, the divine realm, and the human soul's journey.

Judas Iscariot Reimagined

Central to The Gospel of Judas is a revolutionary portrayal of Judas Iscariot. Far from the infamous figure who betrays Christ for silver, Judas emerges as a spiritually enlightened disciple uniquely trusted by Jesus.

According to this text, Judas's act is not a betrayal, but a profound fulfillment of divine necessity—a sacrificial role crucial for humanity's spiritual liberation. This perspective invites readers to reconsider traditional assumptions, offering a deeply symbolic interpretation of events traditionally viewed as historical fact.

In this narrative, Judas is privy to esoteric teachings withheld from other disciples, receiving insights into divine mysteries directly from Jesus. These teachings emphasize the soul's transcendence beyond the physical world, guiding readers toward inner enlightenment and spiritual liberation. Judas's unique understanding underscores themes of sacrifice, duty, and the often misunderstood nature of spiritual destiny.

Exploring Gnostic Mysticism

The Gospel of Judas is deeply embedded within the Gnostic tradition, a diverse religious movement that flourished in the early centuries of Christianity. Gnosticism emphasizes knowledge (gnosis) of spiritual truths as the path to salvation, contrasting sharply with orthodox teachings that emphasize faith and doctrinal adherence. Within this tradition, the physical world is often viewed as a flawed or illusory construct, while true enlightenment lies in recognizing and awakening the divine spark inherent in each individual.

This gospel offers a profound exploration of Gnostic cosmology, vividly describing the intricate relationships among divine beings, spiritual hierarchies, and cosmic forces. It portrays the material world as a shadowy realm governed by lesser spiritual entities, urging followers toward an awakened consciousness that transcends material illusions. By understanding these deeper teachings, readers gain invaluable insights into Gnostic perceptions of the universe, humanity's place within it, and the transformative power of spiritual awareness.

Themes and Teachings

Several transformative themes resonate throughout The Gospel of Judas, each inviting deep contemplation and introspection:

1. The Divine Mission and Destiny

Judas's role, portrayed as divinely appointed rather than maliciously motivated, underscores the complex interplay between destiny, choice, and divine purpose. This gospel challenges simplistic notions of good and evil, inviting readers to ponder the intricate ways divine plans unfold through human actions, even those traditionally perceived as negative.

2. Hidden Wisdom and Enlightenment

Central to Gnostic teachings, this gospel emphasizes the acquisition of hidden wisdom as essential for spiritual liberation. Through Jesus's intimate revelations to Judas, readers are encouraged to pursue deeper spiritual truths that lead to self-awareness, awakening, and ultimate union with the divine.

3. The Nature of the Soul

The Gospel of Judas provides profound insights into the nature of the human soul, its origin, destiny, and relationship to the physical world. It invites readers to recognize their inherent divine essence, emphasizing the importance of inner spiritual awakening over external religious observances or rituals.

4. Reinterpreting Betrayal and Sacrifice

By presenting Judas's actions as acts of ultimate sacrifice and loyalty to divine will, the gospel reframes traditional understandings of betrayal. This reinterpretation challenges readers to reflect on the nature of sacrifice, love, and loyalty within their own spiritual journeys, offering a fresh perspective on familiar narratives.

Modern Relevance and Translation

In today's spiritual landscape, characterized by pluralism, questioning, and individual exploration, The

Gospel of Judas holds exceptional relevance. Its teachings invite readers from all backgrounds—scholars, spiritual seekers, theologians, or simply the curious—to engage critically and personally with profound spiritual questions.

This modern translation ensures clarity and accessibility while preserving the text's rich symbolic depth and mystical complexity. By bridging historical context with contemporary understanding, this adaptation invites readers into a transformative dialogue with ancient wisdom, making these profound teachings deeply relevant for personal growth and spiritual exploration.

Embarking on Your Journey

As you delve into The Gospel of Judas, approach this extraordinary text as both historical artifact and spiritual guide. Allow its teachings to challenge conventional beliefs, provoke deep reflection, and illuminate new paths of understanding. Consider Judas's narrative not merely as an alternative history but as a powerful metaphor for spiritual sacrifice, profound faith, and the complexities of divine-human relationships.

This text invites you to question, reflect, and grow spiritually, urging you toward inner awakening and a deeper appreciation of life's mysteries. The insights you gain here may not only transform your perception of familiar stories but also profoundly influence your personal spiritual journey.

A Call to Enlightenment

The Gospel of Judas is more than an ancient curiosity—it is a vibrant, provocative call to deeper spiritual awareness, self-understanding, and enlightenment. As you engage with its teachings, embrace the complexities, paradoxes, and revelations within. Allow yourself the freedom to explore beyond conventional boundaries, discovering truths that resonate deeply within your spiritual consciousness.

May your journey through this transformative text awaken hidden wisdom, inspire profound insights, and deepen your connection to the divine mysteries at the heart of existence. Let The Gospel of Judas illuminate your path toward spiritual enlightenment, reshaping your understanding of faith, sacrifice, and divine purpose.

Jesus Criticizes the Disciples

One day, Jesus was with his disciples in Judea. He found them sitting together, deeply focused on their prayers. They had gathered in a circle, chanting solemnly as they prayed over the bread. When Jesus approached and saw what they were doing, he smiled softly.

Surprised, the disciples turned to him and asked, "Master, why are you smiling at our prayer? Have we done something wrong? Aren't we honoring God by doing this?"

Jesus looked at them and said, "I am not laughing at you. But you are not doing this because you truly desire it. You do it because you believe it will please your God."

Still confused, the disciples said, "Master, you are the Son of our God!"

Jesus looked at them thoughtfully and asked, "How do you truly know me? I tell you the truth—no generation of people among you will fully understand who I am."

Hearing this, the disciples became uneasy. Their confusion turned into frustration, and they felt anger rise in their hearts, upset by words they could not fully grasp.

But Jesus, knowing their thoughts and how they struggled to understand, spoke gently to them. "Why are you letting anger disturb your peace? Is it your God within you, or the stars that guide you, that have caused this unrest? If any one of you has the strength to bring forth true humanity, let that person stand before me now."

The disciples hesitated, glancing at each other. One by one, they claimed, "We are strong enough," but their doubt was clear, and none of them stood up.

Only Judas Iscariot found the courage to rise, but even he could not meet Jesus' eyes. Instead, he lowered his gaze, unable to face him directly.

Judas finally said, "I know who you are and where you came from. You come from the eternal realm of Barbelo. I am not even worthy to speak the name of the one who sent you."

Jesus, seeing that Judas spoke with sincerity, understood the thoughts stirring in his heart. He said to him, "Step away from the others, and I will share with you the mysteries of the kingdom. But know this: you will not enter the kingdom yourself. Instead, you will feel deep sorrow, because someone else will take your place to complete the twelve before their God."

Judas, troubled but eager to understand, asked, "When will you tell me these things? When will the great day of light come for the future generations?"

But Jesus, having spoken what he intended, withdrew from him and walked away.

Another Generation

The next morning, Jesus appeared again to his disciples. They were eager to ask him questions and said, "Master, where did you go? What were you doing when you suddenly left us?"

Jesus looked at them and said, "I went to another great and holy generation."

Confused, the disciples asked, "Lord, what generation could be greater and holier than us? Surely no such group exists anywhere else!"

When Jesus heard this, he smiled—not to mock them, but because he understood how limited their understanding was. He said, "Why are you struggling to understand the strong and holy generation I speak of? I tell you the truth—no one born into this world will ever see that generation. No army of angels from the heavens has power over it, and no human, bound by flesh, can enter it. The generation I speak of does not come from anything you know or from anything connected to this world."

He paused, giving them a moment to take in his words, then continued, "The generation I visited is not like the one here, which has been corrupted. The people among you belong to a world shaped by the powers and rulers of this earth, forces that control and govern everything you know. But the generation I speak of is beyond all of this. It is untouched, pure, and completely free from the influence of those born into this world."

As they listened, the disciples felt uneasy. His words seemed too vast, too mysterious for them to grasp. A deep silence fell over them. They felt something powerful in what he said, but they could not yet understand its full meaning.

The Disciples' Vision

One day, Jesus came to his disciples, and they greeted him excitedly. They said, "Master, last night we had dreams about you, and what we saw was amazing!"

Jesus looked at them and asked, "Why are you hiding yourselves?"

They answered, "We saw a huge house with a beautiful altar inside. Around the altar stood twelve people—we think they were priests. There was a name written there, but we couldn't read it clearly. A large crowd was gathered in front of the altar, watching the priests perform rituals and accept offerings. We stood there too, trying to understand what was happening."

Jesus asked, "What did you see them doing?"

The disciples explained, "Some of the priests fasted for two weeks at a time. Others sacrificed their own children. Some left their wives behind and acted humble while singing praises. Others had relationships with men, committed murders, and did all kinds of sinful and criminal things. And Master, the people at the altar used your name while doing all of this! The priests filled the altar with blood and the remains of their sacrifices."

After telling him this, the disciples fell silent, disturbed by what they had seen.

Jesus, noticing their fear, said, "Why does this trouble you? I tell you the truth—those priests you saw at the altar are calling upon my name. But my name was written there by people, not by God. They have planted trees in my name, but those trees will never bear fruit."

He continued, "The altar and priests in your dream represent you. You are the ones standing before that altar. That altar belongs to the god you serve, and you are the twelve priests. The animals being sacrificed symbolize the people you mislead. Your leader will stand at that altar and use my name, and many devoted followers will trust in him. After him, another will lead those who give in to sin, another will support those who murder children, another will approve of men lying with men, and yet another will promote fasting, along with every kind of mistake, crime, and impurity.

"Some people say, 'We are equal to the angels,' but they are like falling stars, bringing destruction. It has been said, 'God accepts your sacrifice from the hands of priests.' But these priests serve a spirit of deception, not the Lord of all. On the last day, they will be judged for their actions."

Jesus then said, "Stop offering animal sacrifices on the altar. These sacrifices have already been given to the stars and angels you serve, but they mean nothing. Remove them from your midst so you can see the truth clearly."

The disciples, shaken by his words, pleaded, "Master, cleanse us from the sins we have committed because we were deceived."

Jesus answered, "It is not possible to erase all the mistakes of this generation. No single spring can put out the fire of the entire world, nor can one well provide water for all people. Only a great and steady source can do that. A single lamp cannot light up everything, except for the space it was meant to illuminate. In the same way, one baker cannot feed all of creation."

Hearing this, the disciples cried out, "Master, help us! Take this burden away from us!"

Jesus replied, "Stop resisting me. Each of you has your own star, and in the end, the stars will reclaim what belongs to them. I was not sent to this corrupt generation, but to the strong and incorruptible one. That generation has never been ruled by any enemy or controlled by the stars. Truly, I tell you, the pillar of fire will come quickly, and that incorruptible generation will not be shaken by the stars or anything else."

Jesus and Judas

When Jesus finished speaking to the group, he left, taking Judas Iscariot with him. As they walked, Jesus spoke to Judas in a calm but serious tone.

"The water that flows on the highest mountain does not come from the wells or rivers of this world," Jesus said. "It is not meant to feed the trees that grow corrupt fruit in this realm. Instead, it nourishes God's paradise, keeping the eternal fruit alive—fruit that never spoils. This water ensures that the path of life for the holy generation remains pure and everlasting."

Judas listened carefully, then asked, "Master, what kind of fruit does this generation produce?"

Jesus replied, "Every human soul will one day pass away. But when the chosen ones of this holy generation complete their time in the kingdom, their spirits will leave their earthly bodies behind. While their bodies will die like all others, their souls will live on forever, rising to the higher realms where they will exist eternally."

Still curious, Judas asked, "What about the rest of humanity? What will happen to everyone else?"

Jesus answered, "You cannot plant seeds on dry, rocky ground and expect a harvest. In the same way, the corrupted and mortal wisdom that created ordinary humans cannot bring them to the higher realms. Their souls will remain tied to this world. I tell you the truth—no ruler, no angel, and no power will ever see the place that this great and holy generation will inherit."

After saying this, Jesus stepped away. Judas stood there, deep in thought, then called out, "Master, as you have listened to the others, please listen to me now. I have seen a powerful vision."

Jesus turned back to him and chuckled softly. "Why are you so troubled, Judas, you thirteenth spirit? Speak, and I will listen."

Judas, unfazed by Jesus' words, continued, "In my vision, I saw myself surrounded by the twelve disciples. They were throwing stones at me and chasing me like an enemy. Then, I followed you to a place unlike anything I've ever seen. There was a house so enormous that I couldn't measure it with my eyes. Around it stood great and noble people, and the roof was covered in greenery. Inside, a large crowd had gathered, but I didn't understand why they were there. Master, please take me into this house and let me be among these people!"

Jesus looked at him and said, "Judas, your star has led you astray. No human born into this world can enter the house you saw—it is reserved for the holy and pure. In that place, there is no sun or moon, no day or night. Only those who are truly holy may live there, standing forever among the angels. I have already revealed to you the secrets of the kingdom and the errors of the stars. I have shown you what exists beyond the twelve realms you know."

With growing concern in his voice, Judas asked, "Master, my lineage doesn't rule over these realms, does it?"

Jesus replied, "Come closer, and I will tell you about the holy generation. But understand this—I am not telling you so that you may join them. Instead, you will feel great sorrow when you see the kingdom and its people, knowing that you cannot enter."

Judas, now filled with fear, asked, "Then what was the point of separating me from that generation?"

Jesus answered, "You will become the thirteenth, Judas. The other generations will curse you, and you will rule over them in their error. In the last days, people will turn to you in their confusion, but you will not rise to the holy generation, for it was never meant for you."

Jesus Reveals Everything to Judas

Jesus said, "Come closer, and I will reveal secrets no human has ever seen. There is a vast and endless realm, so great that even the angels cannot reach its boundaries. In this place lives a mighty and invisible Spirit, unseen by any angel, beyond human understanding, and without a name.

"A bright cloud appeared, and from it, the Spirit spoke, saying, 'Let an angel come into being to serve me.' From this cloud, a great angel was born—the Self-Begotten, the God of Light. Because of him, four more angels came from another cloud to serve him. The Self-Begotten then said, 'Let a new realm exist,' and so it was. He created the first great light to rule over it and called forth many angels to serve it.

"Then he said, 'Let another bright realm appear,' and it was created. He brought forth a second great light to rule there and assigned more angels to serve it. He repeated this process again and again, creating many realms of light, each with its own ruler and countless angels.

"In the first cloud of light was Adamas, a being no angel or divine figure could fully perceive. From Adamas came Seth, who was made in the image of the first great angel. From Seth, a pure and unbreakable generation was born. This generation brought forth twelve bright rulers, and these twelve created seventy-two more, as the Spirit willed. Each of the seventy-two produced five more, leading to a total of three hundred sixty rulers, each guiding a part of the twelve great realms.

"These twelve leaders shaped their own realms, each containing six heavens, adding up to seventy-two heavens in total. Each heaven had five firmaments, forming three hundred sixty firmaments. In each of these, there were countless armies of angels and pure spirits assigned to serve.

"This entire assembly is called 'the cosmos,' which the Father and the seventy-two rulers labeled as 'perishable.' Yet within it, the first human appeared, given unbreakable power. This realm also contained the cloud of wisdom and an angel called Eleleth. Eleleth said, 'Let twelve angels come forth to rule over Chaos and the underworld.' From this cloud appeared an angel with a fiery face, stained with blood. His name was

Nebro, meaning 'Rebel,' though others called him Yaldabaoth. Another angel, Saklas, also emerged.

"Nebro created six angels to assist him, and Saklas did the same. Together, they brought forth twelve angels to rule the heavens, each given a share of power. These twelve rulers then decided to make humanity in their own image. Saklas said to his angels, 'Let us create a human being in our likeness.' So, they formed Adam and Eve, who, in the divine realm, is called 'Life,' because all generations seek him. Each generation knows her by a different name.

"Saklas, however, did not give them the ability to create life on their own. Instead, an angel spoke and declared that Adam's days, and those of his children, would be numbered."

Judas then asked Jesus, "Master, how long can a person live?"

Jesus answered, "Why does this surprise you? Adam and his descendants have limited lifespans because they belong to a kingdom ruled by Saklas."

Judas asked, "Does the human spirit die too?"

Jesus replied, "This is how it works: God told Michael to lend spirits to humans so they could live and serve. Later, the Great One ordered Gabriel to give spirits to the pure generation—spirits with souls. The rest of the souls, taken from the light but trapped in Chaos, search for the Spirit within them. It was God who gave Adam and his followers wisdom, so that the rulers of Chaos and the underworld would not have complete control over them."

Judas then asked, "What will happen to those future generations?"

Jesus said, "Listen carefully. The stars guide all things. When Saklas' time is complete, the first star of his generation will rise, and everything that was foretold will happen. These generations will sin in my name, committing terrible acts, harming children, and corrupting the world. They will offer these deeds to Saklas, who will rule over them. Then the twelve tribes of Israel will rise, and all generations will follow Saklas, continuing to sin in my name. And you, Judas, your star will rule over the thirteenth realm."

At this, Jesus laughed.

Judas, feeling uneasy, asked, "Master, why are you laughing at me?"

Jesus answered, "I am not laughing at you, Judas, but at the mistake of the stars. Six stars have fallen, along with five warriors, and what they have created will eventually be destroyed."

Judas then asked, "Master, what will happen to those who have been baptized in your name?"

The Betrayal

Jesus said, "Listen carefully—I tell you the truth, the baptism they have received in my name will bring about the downfall of this entire earthly generation. Tomorrow, they will bring suffering upon the one who carries my spirit. But know this: no human hand will ever truly take hold of me, and no earthly power will ever fully understand who I am.

"Judas, pay attention. Those who offer sacrifices to Saklas believe they are serving something greater, but in reality, they are only feeding the forces of evil. Yet, your actions will surpass all of them, for you will sacrifice the man who carries my spirit. Already, your strength has grown, your anger has been set ablaze, your star has risen, and your heart has strayed from its path.

"I tell you, the end is near. The rulers of this world are falling. The kings who once held power have become weak, and even the angels mourn their failure. The corruption they created is beginning to unravel, and their leader is approaching his destruction. When that moment comes, the chosen ones from the great generation of Adam will rise and be honored. They belong to the eternal realm, existing before heaven, earth, and even the angels were formed.

"Judas, look now—I have shared everything you need to know. Lift your eyes to the heavens and see. There is a radiant cloud of light, and within it, stars shine in a perfect circle. Among them, one star leads the way—that star is yours."

Judas, filled with wonder and fear, looked up and saw the brilliant cloud glowing above. The stars around it sparkled like a celestial choir. Drawn by an unseen force, Judas stepped forward and entered the cloud. As he rose into it, those left on the ground heard a voice echoing from within. Though the words were unclear, they spoke of a powerful generation and a destiny beyond human understanding.

Then, Judas was gone. He could no longer see Jesus, nor could anyone else.

Immediately, unrest spread among the Jewish leaders. The disturbance rippled through their ranks, and the high priests muttered among themselves in frustration. Jesus had gone into a guest room to pray, and they had failed to reach him. Watching closely from the shadows, the scribes waited for the right moment to act. Yet, they hesitated, afraid of the people, for many regarded Jesus as a prophet.

Then, Judas returned. The priests and scribes turned to him, their eyes filled with suspicion. They asked, "Why are you here? Aren't you one of Jesus' disciples?"

Judas hesitated for a moment, then spoke the words they had been hoping for. With his response, they found the confirmation they needed. Soon after, they handed him a sum of money in exchange for what he had done. In that moment, the plan they had been waiting for fell into place, and the events leading to Jesus' fate were set into motion.

Thank You for Reading

Dear Reader,

We hope this timeless classic has sparked your imagination and enriched your literary journey. Now that you've turned the final page, we want to share a vision for the future of reading—one where every classic you've ever wanted to explore is at your fingertips, in a format that best suits your life.

We'd like to invite you to gain immediate, unlimited digital & audiobook access to hundreds of the most treasured literary classics ever written—along with the option to secure deluxe paperback, hardcover & box set editions at printing cost. Together, we can spark a new global literary renaissance alongside our small, independent publishing house called "The Library of Alexandria."

Thousands of years ago, the Library of Alexandria stood as a beacon of knowledge—until it was lost to history. We aim to reignite that spirit of preservation and discovery right now, in the modern age—only this time, it's accessible to all, in every language and every format.

Picture a world where every timeless classic, novel, poem, or philosophical treatise is not only available to read but also updated for today's readers—modernized, translated into any language or dialect, and ready to enjoy in any format you choose, whether that is in an eBook, audiobook, paperback, or deluxe hardcover & box set version a printing cost.

By joining our movement to rebuild the modern Library of Alexandria, you become part of an unprecedented mission to offer:

- **Unlimited Audiobook & eBook Access to the Greatest Classics of All Time**

   Instantly explore thousands of legendary works, from Plato and Shakespeare to Jane Austen and Leo Tolstoy. All are instantly ready to read or listen to, giving you a complete literary universe at your fingertips.

- **Paperback & Deluxe Editions at Printing Costs:**

   Purchase any title in a paperback, deluxe hardbound, or deluxe boxset edition at printing costs, shipped right to your doorstep. Curate your personal library of Alexandria with editions worthy of display—crafted to last, designed to captivate, and delivered straight to your door.

- **Modern translations for Contemporary Readers in all languages and dialects**

  Discover a vast selection of classics reimagined in clear, current language—no more struggling with outdated phrases or obscure references. Next to the original versions, we aim to offer translations in as many languages and dialects as possible.

  As we continue our translation efforts and add new languages, readers everywhere can connect with these works as if they were written today. By bridging linguistic divides, you're contributing to ensuring that these timeless stories become more meaningful, accessible, and inspiring for people across the globe.

- **Your Personal Library of Alexandria:**

  Over the months and years, you'll curate a unique physical archive of classics—each volume a testament to your taste, curiosity, and love of knowledge. It's not just about owning books—it's about curating a cultural legacy you'll cherish and pass down for generations to come.

- **Join a Global Literary Renaissance:**

  Your support fuels an ongoing mission: allowing us to reinvest in offering deluxe print editions (including special boxsets) at their true cost, broaden the range of available formats and translations, and extend the reach of these works to new audiences worldwide. By joining today, you're not just preserving a legacy of masterpieces; you set in motion a powerful wave of literary accessibility.

We are more than a publisher—we're a movement, and we can't do it alone. Your support lets us scale our mission, preserving and reimagining history's greatest works for tomorrow's readers.

Become a Torchbearer of knowledge.

Thank you for picking up this book and allowing us into your literary journey. As you turn the pages, know that you're part of something larger: a global effort to keep these stories alive, share their wisdom across borders and generations, and spark a true cultural revival for the modern era.

If this resonates with you—please consider taking the next step by visiting:

www.libraryofalexandria.com

With gratitude and a shared love of knowledge,

The Modern Library of Alexandria Team

Visit:

www.libraryofalexandria.com

Or scan the code below:

www.ingramcontent.com/pod-product-compliance
Lightning Source LLC
LaVergne TN
LVHW030631080426
835512LV00021B/3462